Betty Crocker's
b e s t
CHRISTMAS
C O O K B O O K

Special Wal-Mart Edition

WILEY

Wiley Publishing, Inc.

GENERAL MILLS, INC.
Betty Crocker Kitchens
Manager, Publishing: Lois L. Tlusty
Editors: Kelly Kilen, Karen Sorensen
Recipe Development: Karen Linden
Food Stylists: Cindy Lund, Carol Grones, Cindy Syme
Nutritionist: Nancy Holmes, R.D.

Photographic Services
Art Director: Emily Oberg
Photographers: Steven B. Olson, Valerie J. Bourassa

WILEY PUBLISHING, INC.
Cover and Interior Design: Michele Laseau and Holly Wittenberg

For consistent baking results, the Betty Crocker Kitchens recommend Gold Medal Flour.

Christmas cheer is contagious!

So I am sharing some of my best ideas with you . . .

In this special "mini" edition of my *Best Christmas Cookbook,* I'm giving you a taste of all the great things you can make for the holidays using the full-sized edition (see page 48)—from decking your halls to sitting down to your Christmas feast.

Every Christmas category is covered—party appetizers and holiday drinks, merry main dishes and sides, delicious desserts and homemade breads, scrumptious cookie and candy recipes, plus food gifts and decorations to make any holiday sparkle. And if you're looking for great ideas, this is the place to be—every recipe in the book is photographed so you'll see exactly what you're making. You'll also find a host of "at a glance" tips and suggestions that will help you make all your festivities shine.

I love entertaining at Christmas and enjoy sharing fun and food with family and friends—cooking and Christmas just go together. So, if you are looking for easy, creative ideas for the holidays, look no further. Let's get started creating some lifelong memories!

Betty Crocker
P.S. Merry Christmas!

CONTENTS

Simple Sippers and Savory Nibbles

Merry Main Dishes

Sensational Salads and Sides

Fabulous Finales

Holiday Eggnog
6

Cinnamon Cider
7

Appetizer Cheese Trees
8

Ginger Shrimp Kabobs
10

Burgundy Beef Stew
12

Glazed Baked Ham
14

Chicken Dijon Casserole
16

Three-Bean Christmas Chili
17

Heavenly Fruit Salad
18

Applesauce–Sweet Potato Bake
20

Broccoli-Corn Casserole
21

Jeweled Fruitcake
22

Heavenly Cheesecake
24

Peanut Brittle Bread Pudding
25

Holiday Breads

Julekake
26

Pesto Biscuits
28

Sweet Shop Favorites

Holiday Spritz
30

Peppermint Bark
32

Chocolate-Wine Balls
33

Oven Caramel Corn
34

Festive Family Fun

Fudgy No-Bakes
35

Christmas Mice
Shortbread
36

North Pole Strawberry
Smoothie
37

Christmas Vacation
Peanut Butter Fondue
38

Holiday Gifts and Decorations

Pineapple-Apricot Jam
40

Spicy Mocha Mix
41

Easy Festive
Peppermint
Marshmallows
42

Salt Dough
Decorations
43

Cranberry Kissing Ball
44

*Helpful Nutrition and
Cooking Information, 45*
Index, 46

Holiday Eggnog

PREP: 10 MIN; COOK: 20 MIN
6 SERVINGS

3 eggs, slightly beaten

1/3 cup granulated sugar

Dash of salt

2 1/2 cups milk

1 teaspoon vanilla

1/2 cup rum, if desired

1 cup whipping (heavy) cream

1 tablespoon packed brown sugar

Ground nutmeg

Mix eggs, granulated sugar and salt in heavy 2-quart saucepan. Gradually stir in milk. Cook over low heat 15 to 20 minutes, stirring constantly, just until mixture coats a metal spoon; remove from heat. Stir in vanilla and rum. Keep warm.

Just before serving, beat whipping cream and brown sugar in chilled small bowl with electric mixer on high speed until stiff. Gently stir 1 cup of the whipped cream into eggnog mixture.

Pour eggnog into small heatproof punch bowl. Drop remaining whipped cream into 4 or 5 mounds onto eggnog. Sprinkle nutmeg on whipped cream mounds. Serve immediately. Cover and refrigerate any remaining eggnog.

1 Serving: Calories 260 (Calories from Fat 155); Fat 17g (Saturated 10g); Cholesterol 160mg; Sodium 100mg; Carbohydrate 20g (Dietary Fiber 0g); Protein 7g
% Daily Value: Vitamin A 18%; Vitamin C 2%; Calcium 16%; Iron 2%
Diet Exchanges: 1 Fruit, 1 Skim Milk

See photo on page 7.

Holiday Hints

EGGNOG FOR EVERYONE!

- For the coffee lovers in your family, make **Hot Cappuccino Eggnog**: Substitute coffee liqueur for the rum and add 1 cup hot espresso coffee. Don't worry if you don't have brewed espresso coffee; any strongly brewed cup of coffee (regular or decaf) will work.

- Freeze small dollops of whipped cream by scooping them out onto a cookie sheet and freezing until firm. Keep them handy in a resealable plastic freezer bag. Place one dollop on each drink just before serving, and sprinkle lightly with ground cinnamon or nutmeg.

- Place plain or chocolate-dipped pirouette cookies in a pretty serving piece for guests to use as edible stirring spoons.

- Love the flavor of eggnog but not the calories? Substitute 2 eggs plus 2 egg whites for the 3 eggs and 2 1/4 cups skim milk for the milk. Instead of the beaten whipping cream and brown sugar, use 2 cups frozen (thawed) whipped topping.

- Don't have time to make your own eggnog? Dress up purchased eggnog instead. Place eggnog in punch bowl, scoop dollops of cinnamon or French vanilla ice cream over the nog and sprinkle with ground nutmeg.

Cinnamon Cider

PREP: 10 MIN; COOK: 25 MIN
32 SERVINGS

1 gallon apple cider

2/3 cup sugar

2 teaspoons whole allspice

2 teaspoons whole cloves

2 cinnamon sticks, 3 inches long

2 oranges, studded with cloves

Heat all ingredients except oranges to boiling in Dutch oven; reduce heat. Cover and simmer 20 minutes.

Strain punch. Pour into small heatproof punch bowl. Float oranges in bowl. Serve hot.

1 Serving: Calories 75 (Calories from Fat 0); Fat 0g (Saturated 0g); Cholesterol 0mg; Sodium 5mg; Carbohydrate 19g (Dietary Fiber 0g); Protein 0g
% Daily Value: Vitamin A 0%; Vitamin C 0%; Calcium 0%; Iron 2%
Diet Exchanges: 1 Fruit

Party Pointers

- Pull out the slow cooker to help you with the holidays. When serving hot cider at a holiday buffet, pour heated cider into slow cooker set on low and let guests help themselves.

- If you prefer to keep the hot cider in the kitchen, invite guests into the kitchen to ladle cider into their own mugs. Use an attractive saucepan kept right on the stove top over low heat.

- You can make a glass punch bowl safer for hot beverages by filling it first with hot water and letting it stand about 30 minutes. Pour out water, and slowly add hot punch.

Holiday Eggnog (page 6) and Cinnamon Cider

Appetizer Cheese Trees

PREP: 30 MIN; CHILL: 4 HR
ABOUT 7 CUPS SPREAD

3 packages (8 ounces each) cream cheese,
softened

4 cups shredded Cheddar cheese
(16 ounces)

2 tablespoons pesto

1 tablespoon grated onion

1/4 teaspoon ground mustard (dry)

2 or 3 drops red pepper sauce

Have ready at serving time:

1/4 cup finely chopped parsley or cilantro

1/4 cup pine nuts

2 tablespoons chopped red bell pepper

Assorted crackers, if desired

Mix cream cheese and Cheddar cheese; divide in
half. Mix pesto into 1 half; mix onion, mustard
and pepper sauce into other half. Cover each
half and refrigerate about 4 hours or until firm
enough to shape.

Place cheese mixtures on cookie sheet. Shape
each half into cone shape to look like Christmas
tree. Roll trees in parsley, pressing parsley evenly
onto trees. Press pine nuts onto trees in string
form for garland. Press bell pepper pieces onto
trees for ornaments. Top each tree with star
shape cut from lemon peel if desired. Serve with
crackers.

1/4 Cup: Calories 155 (Calories from Fat 125); Fat 14g
(Saturated 9g); Cholesterol 45mg; Sodium 180mg; Carbohydrate 1g
(Dietary Fiber 0g); Protein 6g
% Daily Value: Vitamin A 10%; Vitamin C 0%; Calcium 10%; Iron 2%
Diet Exchanges: 1 High-Fat Meat, 1 Fat

Timesaving Tips

This is a great do-ahead appetizer. After shaping
cheese mixtures on the cookie sheet, wrap in plastic
wrap or aluminum foil, label and freeze up to one
month. Twelve hours before serving, remove the
trees from the freezer. Thaw in wrapper in the refrigerator. Continue as directed.

New Twist

Here's an idea the kids will love!
Instead of trees, make snowmen!
Shape the cheese mixture into a
Snowman Cheese Ball (you'll
have enough to make 2 small
snowmen or 1 large one). Omit
parsley, pine nuts and bell
pepper. Mix cream cheese and
Cheddar cheese; divide into

3 equal parts. Mix 2 parts to
equal two-thirds of mixture; mix
in pesto. Mix onion, mustard
and pepper sauce into remaining one-third of cheese mixture.
Refrigerate as directed. Shape
each cheese mixture into
2 balls; roll in 1/3 cup finely
chopped blanched almonds.

Arrange balls on serving plate
with smaller ball on top for
head of snowman; press together
slightly. Insert pretzel sticks
for arms. Decorate as desired
with capers, sliced olives,
chopped carrots, sliced cucum-
ber, chopped bell peppers and
fresh thyme leaves.

Appetizer Cheese Trees and Snowman Cheese Ball (variation)

Ginger Shrimp Kabobs

PREP: 30 MIN; CHILL: 1 HR; BROIL: 6 MIN
12 APPETIZERS

12 uncooked large shrimp in shells

1 tablespoon grated gingerroot

2 tablespoons lime juice

2 teaspoons soy sauce

1 teaspoon dark sesame oil

1/4 teaspoon crushed red pepper

3 cloves garlic, finely chopped

2 medium bell peppers

12 small whole mushrooms

6 green onions, cut into 1-inch pieces

Peel shrimp. (If shrimp are frozen, do not thaw; peel in cold water.) Make a shallow cut lengthwise down back of each shrimp; wash out vein.

Mix gingerroot, lime juice, soy sauce, sesame oil, red pepper and garlic in glass or plastic dish. Stir in shrimp until well coated. Cover and refrigerate 1 hour.

Cut bell peppers with small star-shaped cookie cutter, or cut into 1-inch squares.

Set oven to broil. Remove shrimp from marinade; reserve marinade. Alternate bell pepper star, mushroom, shrimp and onion pieces on each of twelve 6-inch skewers. Brush lightly with marinade. Place on rack in broiler pan.

Broil with tops about 4 inches from heat about 6 minutes, turning once, until shrimp are pink and firm and vegetables are crisp-tender. Discard remaining marinade.

1 Appetizer: Calories 25 (Calories from Fat 10); Fat 1g (Saturated 0g); Cholesterol 15mg; Sodium 70mg; Carbohydrate 3g (Dietary Fiber 1g); Protein 2g
% Daily Value: Vitamin A 2%; Vitamin C 16%; Calcium 0%; Iron 2%
Diet Exchanges: 1 Vegetable

Timesaving Tips

You can make these kabobs ahead of time. Cover and refrigerate prepared kabobs up to 24 hours ahead, then they'll be ready to pop under the broiler when your guests arrive.

Party Pointers

If you are having a large group and the guests may not know one another, consider having each guest wear a name tag. This helps people remember each other and puts people at ease if they've forgotten the name of someone they have just met.

Ginger Shrimp Kabobs

Burgundy Beef Stew

PREP: 25 MIN; COOK: 1 HR 40 MIN
8 SERVINGS

6 slices bacon, cut into 1-inch pieces

2-pound beef boneless chuck eye, rolled
    rump or bottom round roast, cut into
    1-inch pieces

1/2 cup all-purpose flour

1 1/2 cups dry red wine or beef broth

1 1/2 teaspoons chopped fresh or
    1/2 teaspoon dried thyme leaves

1 1/4 teaspoons salt

1 teaspoon beef bouillon granules

1/4 teaspoon pepper

1 clove garlic, chopped

1 bay leaf

2 tablespoons butter or margarine

1 package (8 ounces) sliced mushrooms

4 medium onions, sliced

Chopped fresh parsley, if desired

Cook bacon in Dutch oven over medium heat until crisp; drain, reserving fat in Dutch oven. Drain bacon on paper towels; crumble bacon.

Coat beef with flour. Cook beef in bacon fat over medium heat, stirring occasionally, until brown. Drain excess fat from Dutch oven. Add wine and just enough water to cover beef. Stir in thyme, salt, bouillon granules, pepper, garlic and bay leaf. Heat to boiling; reduce heat. Cover and simmer about 1 1/2 hours or until beef is tender.

Melt butter in 12-inch skillet over medium heat. Cook mushrooms and onions in butter, stirring occasionally, until onions are tender. Stir mushroom mixture and bacon into beef mixture. Cover and simmer 10 minutes. Remove bay leaf. Garnish stew with parsley.

1 Serving: Calories 260 (Calories from Fat 115); Fat 13g (Saturated 5g); Cholesterol 45mg; Sodium 680mg; Carbohydrate 13g (Dietary Fiber 1g); Protein 17g
% Daily Value: Vitamin A 4%; Vitamin C 4%; Calcium 2%; Iron 14%
Diet Exchanges: 2 High-Fat Meat, 2 Vegetable

Timesaving Tips

When schedules are hectic and appetites are hearty, use one of these techniques to get dinner cooking while you take care of other projects:

- Cook recipe in a slow cooker. Follow the manufacturer's directions for your slow cooker for cooking times. Stews usually cook on the low heat setting for 6 to 8 hours.

- Cook stew in a 325° oven in an ovenproof Dutch oven for about 4 hours.

Burgundy Beef Stew

Glazed Baked Ham

PREP: 10 MIN; BAKE: 13 TO 17 MIN PER POUND; STAND: 10 MIN
12 TO 16 SERVINGS

6- to 8-pound fully cooked bone-in ham

Whole cloves, if desired

1/4 cup honey

1/2 teaspoon ground mustard (dry)

1/4 teaspoon ground cloves

Heat oven to 325°. Place ham, fat side up, on rack in shallow roasting pan. Insert meat thermometer so tip is in thickest part of ham and does not touch bone or rest in fat. Cover ham and bake 13 to 17 minutes per pound or until thermometer reads 135°: 6-pound ham, 1 hour 18 minutes to 1 hour 42 minutes; 7-pound ham, 1 hour 31 minutes to 2 hours; 8-pound ham, 1 hour 44 minutes to 2 hours 16 minutes.

About 20 minutes before ham is done, remove from oven. Pour drippings from pan. Remove any skin from ham. Cut uniform diamond shapes on fat surface of ham. Insert clove in each diamond. Mix honey, mustard and cloves; brush over ham. Bake uncovered 20 minutes.

Cover ham loosely with aluminum foil tent and let stand about 10 minutes or until thermometer reads 140°.

1 Serving: Calories 175 (Calories from Fat 55); Fat 6g (Saturated 2g); Cholesterol 60mg; Sodium 1,310mg; Carbohydrate 7g (Dietary Fiber 0g); Protein 23g
% Daily Value: Vitamin A 0%; Vitamin C 0%; Calcium 0%; Iron 8%
Diet Exchanges: 2 1/2 Lean Meat, 1/2 Fruit

Holiday Hints

CARVING BONE-IN HAM

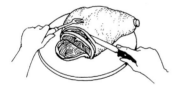

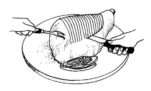

a. Letting the roast stand for 10 minutes allows the juices to set up and makes carving easier. Place ham, fat side up and bone to your right, on carving board. Cut a few slices from the thin side. Turn ham cut side down, so it rests firmly.

b. Make vertical slices down to the leg bone, then cut horizontally along bone to release slices.

Timesaving Tips

If you like the convenience of a presliced ham, ask your meat retailer to cut the ham, reassemble it and tie with cord. You still can use the same wonderful glaze.

New Twist

Looking for a new festive finish for baked ham? Try one of these suggestions:

- **Honey of a Sauce:** Mix 6 table-spoons honey mustard and 1 cup sour cream.

- **Sour Cherry Sauce:** Mix 1/4 cup packed brown sugar, 1 tablespoon cornstarch and 1/2 teaspoon ground mustard (dry) in 1-quart saucepan. Stir in 1/2 cup dried sour cherries, 3/4 cup water, 1/2 teaspoon grated lemon peel and 2 tablespoons lemon juice. Cook over low heat 6 to 8 minutes, stirring constantly, until thickened.

- **Raisin Sauce:** Mix 1/2 cup packed brown sugar, 2 tablespoons cornstarch and 1 teaspoon ground mustard (dry) in 1-quart saucepan. Gradually stir in 1 1/4 cups water and 2 table-spoons lemon juice. Stir in 1 cup raisins. Cook over medium heat, stirring constantly, until mixture boils. Boil and stir 1 minute.

Glazed Baked Ham

Chicken Dijon Casserole

PREP: 30 MIN; BAKE: 30 MIN

6 SERVINGS

3 cups uncooked farfalle (bow-tie) pasta
(6 ounces)

2 cups cubed cooked chicken

1/3 cup diced roasted red bell peppers
(from 7-ounce jar)

2 cups frozen broccoli cuts
(from 16-ounce bag)

1 can (10 3/4 ounces) condensed cream of
chicken or cream of mushroom soup

1/3 cup chicken broth

3 tablespoons Dijon mustard

1 tablespoon finely chopped onion

1/2 cup shredded Parmesan cheese

Heat oven to 375°. Grease 2 1/2-quart casserole.
Cook and drain pasta as directed on package.

Mix pasta, chicken, bell peppers and broccoli in
casserole. Mix soup, broth, mustard and onion;
stir into pasta mixture. Sprinkle with cheese.

Cover and bake about 30 minutes or until mixture is hot and cheese is melted.

1 Serving: Calories 400 (Calories from Fat 90); Fat 10g
(Saturated 3g); Cholesterol 50mg; Sodium 690mg; Carbohydrate 53g
(Dietary Fiber 3g); Protein 27g
% Daily Value: Vitamin A 12%; Vitamin C 20%; Calcium 14%;
Iron 20%
Diet Exchanges: 3 Starch, 2 Medium-Fat Meat, 1 Vegetable

Chicken Dijon Casserole

Holiday Hints

- Use fresh broccoli instead of
frozen; add it to the boiling
pasta during the last 2 to 3
minutes of cooking.

- Add a splash of wine! Use
1/3 cup dry white wine
instead of the chicken broth.

- Make this recipe your way
by using your favorite pasta
or the one available in your
cupboard.

Three-Bean Christmas Chili

PREP: 15 MIN; COOK: 25 MIN
6 SERVINGS

1 can (28 ounces) whole tomatoes, undrained

1 can (15 to 16 ounces) garbanzo beans, drained

1 can (15 to 16 ounces) kidney beans, drained

1 can (15 to 16 ounces) butter beans, drained

1 can (15 ounces) tomato sauce

3 small red, orange or yellow bell peppers, cut into 1-inch pieces

1 Anaheim or jalapeño chili, seeded and chopped

1 to 2 tablespoons chili powder

2 teaspoons ground cumin

1/4 teaspoon pepper

1/2 cup sour cream

3 tablespoons salsa

Chopped fresh cilantro, if desired

Mix all ingredients except sour cream and salsa in Dutch oven. Heat to boiling, breaking up tomatoes; reduce heat. Cover and simmer 15 to 20 minutes or until bell peppers are tender.

Mix sour cream and salsa. Serve chili with sour cream mixture. Sprinkle with cilantro.

1 Serving: Calories 265 (Calories from Fat 45); Fat 5g (Saturated 2g); Cholesterol 10mg; Sodium 820mg; Carbohydrate 50g (Dietary Fiber 14g); Protein 16g
% Daily Value: Vitamin A 28%; Vitamin C 72%; Calcium 12%; Iron 34%
Diet Exchanges: 3 Starch, 1 Vegetable

Party Pointers

Invite the gang over for a tree-trimming party. Double the chili recipe, make it in a 6-quart Dutch oven and serve a "make it your way" chili bar. Provide toppings of sour cream, salsa, shredded cheeses, chopped red onion, chopped ripe olives, chopped avocado and, for the bold, red pepper sauce. Have baskets filled with croutons, tortilla chips, crackers, muffins and breadsticks for chili dipping. For an extra treat, offer purchased bread bowls or tortilla bowls (available at your supermarket) to serve the chili in.

Three-Bean Christmas Chili

Heavenly Fruit Salad

PREP: 20 MIN
6 SERVINGS

Orange-Honey Dressing (right)

1 medium jicama, peeled and cut into
1/4-inch slices

3 oranges, peeled and sliced

3 kiwifruit, peeled and sliced

1/4 cup pomegranate seeds or dried
cranberries

Orange-Honey Dressing

1/4 cup orange juice

1/4 cup honey

1/2 teaspoon ground cinnamon

Shake all ingredients in tightly covered container.

Prepare Orange-Honey Dressing. Cut jicama
slices with star-shaped cookie cutter.

Mix jicama, oranges and kiwifruit in serving
bowl. Toss with dressing. Sprinkle with pomegranate seeds.

1 Serving: Calories 110 (Calories from Fat 0); Fat 0g (Saturated 0g);
Cholesterol 0mg; Sodium 5mg; Carbohydrate 32g (Dietary Fiber 6g);
Protein 2g
% Daily Value: Vitamin A 2%; Vitamin C 100%; Calcium 4%; Iron 4%
Diet Exchanges: 2 Fruit

Holiday Hints

POMEGRANATE POINTERS

Bright red pomegranate seeds add a holiday finishing touch to any salad. Pomegranates are larger than apples and have a leathery, deep red to purplish red rind. Though not beautiful on the outside, they have a spectacular interior packed full of sparkling, juicy, ruby-colored seeds that are slightly sweet and refreshingly tart.

To remove the seeds, cut the knobby end off the pomegranate, and score the rind lengthwise four to six times. Place the pomegranate in a bowl and cover with cool water; let stand 5 minutes. Holding the pomegranate under the water, break it apart into sections, separating the seeds from the pithy white membrane. The edible seeds will sink to the bottom of

the bowl, and the bitter, inedible membrane will float to the top. Discard the membrane and the rind. Drain the seeds in a colander, then gently pat dry with paper towels. Be careful when doing this process because the juice can stain permanently.

Heavenly Fruit Salad

Applesauce–Sweet Potato Bake

PREP: 45 MIN; BAKE: 30 MIN

6 SERVINGS

1 pound sweet potatoes or yams
(about 3 medium)

1 cup applesauce

1/3 cup packed brown sugar

1/4 cup chopped nuts

1/2 teaspoon ground cinnamon

2 tablespoons butter or margarine

Place sweet potatoes in 3-quart saucepan; add enough water (salted if desired) to cover. Heat to boiling; reduce heat. Cover and simmer 30 to 35 minutes or until tender; drain. Remove skins; cut each sweet potato lengthwise in half.

Heat oven to 375°. Place sweet potatoes, cut sides up, in ungreased 2-quart casserole or square baking dish, 8×8×2 inches. Spread applesauce over sweet potatoes. Mix brown sugar, nuts and cinnamon; sprinkle over applesauce. Dot with butter. Cover and bake about 30 minutes or until hot.

1 Serving: Calories 185 (Calories from Fat 65); Fat 7g (Saturated 3g); Cholesterol 10mg; Sodium 75mg; Carbohydrate 32g (Dietary Fiber 3g); Protein 2g
% Daily Value: Vitamin A 100%; Vitamin C 12%; Calcium 4%; Iron 4%
Diet Exchanges: 1 Starch, 1 Fruit, 1 Fat

Holiday Hints

Why not try some sweet potato sprinkles?

- Dried cranberries
- Miniature marshmallows
- Canned sliced peaches or pineapple
- Toasted pecans or almonds
- French-fried onion rings or crushed croutons

Timesaving Tips

Looking for a shortcut? Use 1 can (18 ounces) vacuum-packed sweet potatoes, cut lengthwise in half, for the fresh sweet potatoes.

Applesauce–Sweet Potato Bake

Broccoli-Corn Casserole

PREP: 15 MIN; BAKE: 1 HR

8 SERVINGS

2 bags (16 ounces each) frozen broccoli
  flowerets, thawed and drained

2 cans (14 3/4 ounces each) cream-style
  corn

2 eggs, slightly beaten

2 tablespoons butter or margarine, melted

3/4 cup herb-seasoned stuffing crumbs

Heat oven to 350°. Mix broccoli, corn and eggs
in ungreased 3-quart casserole or rectangular
baking dish, 13×9×2 inches. Mix butter and
stuffing; sprinkle evenly over vegetable mixture.

Bake uncovered about 1 hour or until stuffing is
golden and vegetables are hot.

1 Serving: Calories 200 (Calories from Fat 55); Fat 6g (Saturated 3g);
Cholesterol 60mg; Sodium 670mg; Carbohydrate 33g (Dietary
Fiber 5g); Protein 9g
% Daily Value: Vitamin A 24%; Vitamin C 40%; Calcium 8%;
Iron 12%
Diet Exchanges: 1 Starch, 3 Vegetable, 1 Fat

Broccoli-Corn Casserole

Gifts for Giving

Broccoli-Corn Casserole in a new casserole dish
makes a delicious and unique gift for a nearby
neighbor or friend. Prepare the recipe in the casserole dish to give, but save the baking for the gift
recipient. Cover the casserole tightly with plastic
wrap, and include the instructions for baking (you
can even include the entire recipe, if you like).
Wrap it with a bow, and your gift is ready to go!

Jeweled Fruitcake

PREP: 20 MIN; BAKE: 1 3/4 HR; COOL: 1 HR

16 SERVINGS

2 cups dried apricot halves

2 cups pitted whole dates (not sugar coated)

1 1/2 cups Brazil nuts

1 cup red or green candied pineapple, chopped

1 cup red or green whole maraschino cherries, drained

3/4 cup all-purpose flour

3/4 cup sugar

1/2 teaspoon baking powder

1/2 teaspoon salt

1 1/2 teaspoons vanilla

3 eggs

1 tablespoon corn syrup, if desired

Heat oven to 300°. Line loaf pan, 9 × 5 × 3 or 8 1/2 × 4 1/2 × 2 1/2 inches, with aluminum foil; grease foil. Mix all ingredients except corn syrup. Spread in pan.

Bake about 1 3/4 hours or until toothpick inserted in center comes out clean. If necessary, cover with aluminum foil during last 30 minutes of baking to prevent excessive browning. Remove from pan to wire rack.

For a glossy top, brush top with corn syrup. Cool completely. Wrap in plastic wrap; store in refrigerator.

1 Serving: Calories 290 (Calories from Fat 90); Fat 10g (Saturated 2g); Cholesterol 40mg; Sodium 110mg; Carbohydrate 50g (Dietary Fiber 5g); Protein 5g
% Daily Value: Vitamin A 18%; Vitamin C 0%; Calcium 6%; Iron 12%
Diet Exchanges: 1 Starch, 2 1/2 Fruit, 1 Fat

Gifts for Giving

Over the years, fruitcake in America has taken its share of bad jokes, but along the way, some wonderful recipes—like this one—have evolved, full of fruits and nuts bound together with a sweet batter. If you plan on giving fruitcake as a gift or as part of a gift basket, you may like to try Petite Fruitcakes or Mini-Loaves.

Petite Fruitcakes: Place paper or foil baking cup in each of 24 medium muffin cups, 2 1/2 × 1 1/4 inches. Divide batter evenly among cups (about 1/3 cup each). Bake 35 to 40 minutes or until toothpick inserted in center comes out clean. Remove from pan to wire rack. Makes 24 servings.

Mini-Loaves: Generously grease 7 or 8 miniature loaf pans, 4 1/2 × 2 3/4 × 1 1/4 inches, or line with aluminum foil and grease. Divide batter evenly among pans (about 1 cup each). Bake about 1 hour or until toothpick inserted in center comes out clean. Remove from pans to wire rack. Makes 7 or 8 mini-loaves.

Jeweled Fruitcake

Heavenly Cheesecake

PREP: 40 MIN; BAKE: 1 HR; COOL: 15 MIN; CHILL: 8 HR
16 SERVINGS

1 cup vanilla or chocolate wafer cookie or gingersnap cookie crumbs

2 tablespoons butter or margarine, melted

3 packages (8 ounces each) cream cheese, softened

1/2 cup sugar

3 eggs

1 teaspoon vanilla

1 package (12 ounces) white baking chips (2 cups), melted

1/2 cup half-and-half

Cut-up fresh strawberries, if desired

Fresh mint leaves, if desired

Heat oven to 325°. Mix cookie crumbs and butter. Press evenly in bottom of springform pan, 10×3 or 9×3 inches. Refrigerate while preparing filling.

Beat cream cheese in large bowl with electric mixer on medium speed until smooth. Gradually beat in sugar until smooth. Beat in eggs, one at a time. Beat in vanilla, melted baking chips and half-and-half until blended. Pour over crust; smooth top.

New Twist

If you're the kind of baker who likes to add your own touch, try stirring in 1/2 cup of these favorites:

- Miniature semisweet chocolate chips
- Chopped candied fruits
- Choppped dried cranberries or dried cherries
- Chopped hazelnuts or pecans
- Crushed hard peppermint candies

Bake 55 to 60 minutes or until center is set; cool 15 minutes. Run metal spatula around side of cheesecake to loosen. Cover and refrigerate at least 8 hours, but no longer than 48 hours. Remove side of pan. Top cheesecake with strawberries. Garnish with mint leaves. Cover and refrigerate any remaining cheesecake.

1 Serving: Calories 380 (Calories from Fat 235); Fat 26g (Saturated 15g); Cholesterol 95mg; Sodium 190mg; Carbohydrate 32g (Dietary Fiber 1g); Protein 6g
% Daily Value: Vitamin A 16%; Vitamin C 10%; Calcium 8%; Iron 6%
Diet Exchanges: Not Recommended

Heavenly Cheesecake

Peanut Brittle Bread Pudding

PREP: 20 MIN; BAKE: 30 MIN
6 SERVINGS

4 cups soft bread cubes (4 to 5 slices bread)

1/2 cup coarsely broken peanut brittle

1 egg

1/2 cup milk

1/2 cup packed brown sugar

1/4 cup butter or margarine, melted

Hot Buttered Rum Sauce (below)

Whipped cream, if desired

Heat oven to 350°. Grease 1-quart casserole. Place 2 cups of the bread cubes in casserole. Sprinkle with half of the peanut brittle; repeat with remaining bread cubes and peanut brittle.

Beat egg in small bowl. Stir in milk, brown sugar and butter; pour over bread mixture.

Bake uncovered 25 to 30 minutes or until golden brown. Prepare Hot Buttered Rum Sauce. Serve warm pudding with sauce and whipped cream.

1 Serving: Calories 565 (Calories from Fat 325); Fat 36g (Saturated 21g); Cholesterol 130mg; Sodium 3,300mg; Carbohydrate 55g (Dietary Fiber 1g); Protein 6g
% Daily Value: Vitamin A 26%; Vitamin C 0%; Calcium 10%; Iron 8%
Diet Exchanges: Not Recommended

Peanut Brittle Bread Pudding

Hot Buttered Rum Sauce

1/2 cup packed brown sugar

1/2 cup butter or margarine, softened

2/3 cup whipping (heavy) cream

1/4 cup rum or 3 tablespoons water
plus 2 teaspoons rum extract

Mix all ingredients in 2-quart saucepan. Heat to boiling over high heat, stirring constantly. Boil 3 to 4 minutes, stirring constantly, until slightly thickened. Serve warm. Store covered in refrigerator up to 1 week. Sauce may separate during storage; stir before serving.

Holiday Hints

Warm their hearts with this homey dessert. Instead of making the rum sauce, drizzle purchased chocolate syrup over warm pudding, and sprinkle with extra crushed peanut brittle.

Julekake

PREP: 25 MIN; RISE: 2 1/4 HR; BAKE: 40 MIN
1 LOAF (16 SLICES)

1 package regular or quick active dry yeast

1/4 cup very warm water (120° to 130°)

3/4 cup very warm milk (120° to 130°)

1/2 cup sugar

2 tablespoons shortening

1/2 teaspoon salt

1/2 teaspoon ground cardamom

1 egg

1/2 cup raisins

1/3 cup fruitcake mix (mixed candied fruit)

3 1/4 to 3 3/4 cups bread flour or
all-purpose flour

1 egg yolk

2 tablespoons water

Dissolve yeast in warm water in large bowl. Stir in warm milk, sugar, shortening, salt, cardamom, egg, raisins, fruit cake mix and 1 1/2 cups of the flour. Beat with spoon until smooth. Stir in enough remaining flour to make dough easy to handle.

Turn dough onto lightly floured surface. Knead about 5 minutes or until smooth and elastic. Place in greased bowl; turn greased side up. Cover and let rise in warm place about 1 1/2 hours or until double. (Dough is ready if indentation remains when touched.)

Grease round pan, 9 × 1 1/2 inches. Punch down dough. Shape into round loaf. Place in pan. Cover and let rise in warm place about 45 minutes or until double.

Heat oven to 350°. Beat egg yolk and 2 table-spoons water; brush over dough. Bake 30 to 40 minutes or until golden brown.

1 Slice: Calories 195 (Calories from Fat 45); Fat 5g (Saturated 3g); Cholesterol 30mg; Sodium 240mg; Carbohydrate 35g (Dietary Fiber 1g); Protein 4g
% Daily Value: Vitamin A 4%; Vitamin C 0%; Calcium 2%; Iron 10%
Diet Exchanges: 1 Starch, 1 Fruit, 1 Fat

Julekake Bread Machine Variation

1 egg plus enough water to equal 1 cup
plus 2 tablespoons

1/2 teaspoon ground cardamom

1 teaspoon salt

1 tablespoon plus 1 teaspoon sugar

1/4 cup butter, softened*

3 cups bread flour

1 teaspoon bread machine yeast

1/3 cup raisins

1/3 cup fruitcake mix (mixed candied fruit)

Make this recipe with bread machines that use 3 cups flour.

Measure carefully, placing all ingredients except raisins and fruitcake mix in bread machine pan in the order recommended by the manufacturer. Add raisins and fruit cake mix at the raisin/nut signal or 5 to 10 minutes before last kneading cycle ends.

Select Basic/White cycle. Use Medium or Light crust color.

Do not use delay cycles. Remove baked bread from pan, and cool on wire rack.

*We do not recommend margarine for this recipe.

Julekake

Pesto Biscuits

PREP: 15 MIN; BAKE: 12 MIN
10 BISCUITS

2 cups all-purpose flour

3 teaspoons baking powder

1/2 teaspoon salt

1/3 cup shortening

1/4 cup pesto

About 1/2 cup milk

Finely shredded Parmesan cheese,
   if desired

Red or green hot pepper (jalapeño) jelly,
   if desired

Heat oven to 450°. Mix flour, baking powder and salt in large bowl. Cut in shortening and pesto, using pastry blender or crisscrossing 2 knives, until mixture looks like fine crumbs. Stir in just enough milk so dough leaves side of bowl and forms a ball.

Turn dough onto lightly floured surface. Knead lightly 10 times. Roll or pat 1/2 inch thick. Cut with floured 2 1/2-inch cookie or biscuit cutter. Place about 1 inch apart on ungreased cookie sheet. Sprinkle with cheese.

Bake 10 to 12 minutes or until golden brown. Immediately remove from cookie sheet. Serve warm with pepper jelly.

1 Biscuit: Calories 235 (Calories from Fat 100); Fat 11g (Saturated 3g); Cholesterol 0mg; Sodium 320mg; Carbohydrate 30g (Dietary Fiber 1g); Protein 5g
% Daily Value: Vitamin A 0%; Vitamin C 0%; Calcium 12%; Iron 10%
Diet Exchanges: 2 Starch, 2 Fat

Holiday Hints

It's easy to get even your butter into the act of being festive. Slice chilled butter 1/4 inch thick and cut slices with mini-cookie cutters. Use cutters with open tops so you can push the butter through. Simple shapes work best (such as stars, hearts, etc.). Place butter on waxed paper;

refrigerate until ready to serve. Butter scraps can be softened and reshaped or used in baking.

To make large butter pats, place a 3-inch cookie cutter on a plate; fill with softened butter or margarine, spreading even with top of cutter. To unmold, run a knife

dipped in hot water along the inside of cookie cutter, and remove the cutter.

Refrigerate butter shapes until ready to serve, or wrap in colorful plastic wrap, tie with bow and refrigerate until ready to give as a gift with homemade breads.

Pesto Biscuits

Holiday Spritz

PREP: 25 MIN; BAKE: 8 MIN PER SHEET; COOL: 30 MIN

ABOUT 5 DOZEN COOKIES

1 cup butter or margarine, softened

1/2 cup sugar

1 egg

2 1/2 cups all-purpose flour

1/4 teaspoon salt

1/4 teaspoon almond extract or vanilla

Few drops of food color, if desired

Heat oven to 400°. Beat butter, sugar and egg in large bowl with electric mixer on medium speed, or mix with spoon. Stir in remaining ingredients.

Place dough in cookie press. Form desired shapes on ungreased cookie sheet.

Bake 5 to 8 minutes or until set but not brown. Immediately remove from cookie sheet to wire rack; cool completely.

1 Cookie: Calories 50 (Calories from Fat 25); Fat 3g (Saturated 2g); Cholesterol 10mg; Sodium 30mg; Carbohydrate 5g (Dietary Fiber 0g); Protein 1g
% Daily Value: Vitamin A 2%; Vitamin C 0%; Calcium 0%; Iron 0%
Diet Exchanges: 1/2 Starch

CHOCOLATE SPRITZ: Stir 2 ounces unsweetened baking chocolate, melted and cooled, into butter-sugar mixture. Omit food color.

RUM BUTTER SPRITZ: Substitute rum extract for the almond extract. Tint dough with food colors. After baking, spread cooled cookies with **Butter Rum Glaze**: Melt 1/4 cup butter or margarine in 1-quart saucepan; remove from heat. Stir in 1 cup powdered sugar and 1 teaspoon rum extract. Stir in 1 to 2 tablespoons hot water until glaze is spreadable. Tint glaze with food color to match cookies.

SPICY SPRITZ: Stir in 1 teaspoon ground cinnamon, 1/2 teaspoon ground nutmeg and 1/4 teaspoon ground allspice with the flour.

Holiday Hints

Before baking spruce up your Spritz with:

- Currants, raisins, small candies, chopped nuts, slices of candied fruits or candied fruit peels arranged in festive patterns.

After baking decorate with:

- Edible glitter, colored sugar, nonpareils, red cinnamon candies or finely chopped nuts. A drop of corn syrup will hold the decorations in place nicely.

Holiday Spritz

Peppermint Bark

PREP: 15 MIN; STAND: 1 HR
ABOUT 16 CANDIES

1 package (16 ounces) vanilla-flavored candy
  coating (almond bark), broken into pieces
24 hard peppermint candies

Cover cookie sheet with waxed paper, aluminum
foil or cooking parchment paper. Place candy
coating in 8-cup microwavable measure or 2-quart
microwavable casserole. Microwave uncovered
on High 2 to 3 minutes, stirring every 30 seconds,
until almost melted. Stir until smooth.

Place peppermint candies in heavy plastic bag;
crush with rolling pin or bottom of small heavy
saucepan. Pour crushed candies into wire strainer.
Shake strainer over melted coating until all of
the tiniest candy pieces fall into the coating;
reserve the larger candy pieces. Stir coating to
mix evenly.

Spread coating evenly on cookie sheet. Sprinkle
evenly with remaining candy pieces. Let stand
about 1 hour or until cool and hardened. Break
into pieces.

1 Candy: Calories 40 (Calories from Fat 20); Fat 2g (Saturated 2g);
Cholesterol 0mg; Sodium 5mg; Carbohydrate 6g (Dietary Fiber 0g);
Protein 0g
% Daily Value: Vitamin A 0%; Vitamin C 0%; Calcium 2%; Iron 0%
Diet Exchanges: 1/2 Starch

Holiday Hints

Several brands of candy coating are available, and
each may melt a bit differently. The white color
varies, and when melted, some are thinner than
others. Make a note of the brand you prefer to
work with, and watch carefully while melting.

New Twist

Let your imagination run wild!
Leave out the crushed peppermint
candy, and try some of the fol-
lowing combinations:

- Chocolate-
  covered
  coffee beans
  and chopped
  hazelnuts

- Dried cran-
  berries and
  chopped
  almonds

- Crushed red
  and green
  ring-shaped
  hard candy

- Chopped candied
  pineapple and
  macadamia
  nuts

- Red and green plain or
  mint candy-coated
  chocolate
  candies

Chocolate-Wine Balls

PREP: 20 MIN
ABOUT 3 1/2 DOZEN CANDIES

1/4 cup honey

1 package (6 ounces) semisweet chocolate chips (1 cup)

2 1/2 cups finely crushed vanilla wafer cookies (about 55 cookies)

2 cups ground walnuts

1/3 cup port, sweet red wine or apple juice

About 1/2 cup coarse sugar crystals (decorating sugar)

Heat honey and chocolate chips in 3-quart saucepan over low heat, stirring constantly, until chocolate is melted; remove from heat. Stir in crushed cookies, walnuts and port. Shape into 1-inch balls; roll in sugar crystals.

Store in tightly covered container. Let stand several days to blend flavors. Flavor improves with age up to 4 weeks.

1 Candy: Calories 75 (Calories from Fat 35); Fat 4g (Saturated 1g); Cholesterol 0mg; Sodium 15mg; Carbohydrate 10g (Dietary Fiber 1g); Protein 1g
% Daily Value: Vitamin A 0%; Vitamin C 0%; Calcium 0%; Iron 2%
Diet Exchanges: 1/2 Starch, 1 Fat

WHITE WINE BALLS: Omit chocolate chips and do not heat honey. Substitute dry white wine for the port. Mix all ingredients except sugar. Shape into 1-inch balls; roll in sugar. Continue as directed.

RUM BALLS OR BOURBON BALLS: Just substitute rum or bourbon for the port. Prepare as directed.

Gifts for Giving

To give as a gift, wrap candies individually in colorful plastic wrap or cellophane, and tie with metallic ribbons. Fill a wine glass with candies, and be sure to include the candy recipe with your gift.

Chocolate-Wine Balls

Oven Caramel Corn

PREP: 25 MIN; BAKE: 1 HR
ABOUT 15 CUPS CARAMEL CORN

15 cups popped popcorn (about 2/3 cup
  unpopped)

1 cup packed brown sugar

1/2 cup butter or margarine

1/4 cup light corn syrup

1/2 teaspoon salt

1/2 teaspoon baking soda

Heat oven to 200°. Divide popcorn between
2 ungreased rectangular pans, 13×9×2 inches.
Heat brown sugar, butter, corn syrup and salt in
3-quart saucepan over medium heat, stirring
occasionally, until bubbly around edges. Cook
5 minutes, stirring occasionally; remove from
heat. Stir in baking soda.

Pour mixture over popcorn; stir until well coated.
Bake 1 hour, stirring every 15 minutes.

1 Cup: Calories 180 (Calories from Fat 80); Fat 9g (Saturated 4g);
Cholesterol 15mg; Sodium 270mg; Carbohydrate 25g (Dietary
Fiber 1g); Protein 1g
% Daily Value: Vitamin A 4%; Vitamin C 0%; Calcium 2%; Iron 2%
Diet Exchanges: 1 1/2 Starch, 1 1/2 Fat

New Twist

Surprise your family and those on your gift list
with some new flavor twists. Use 12 cups popped
popcorn; toss with ingredients (below) after stirring in brown sugar mixture. Bake as directed.

- **Caramel-Apple Oven Caramel Corn:** Divide
  2 cups dried apple slices, coarsely chopped, and
  1 1/2 cups caramels, cut into fourths, between
  each pan of popcorn.

- **Hawaiian Oven Caramel Corn:** Divide
  1 1/2 cups dried tropical fruit mix and 1 cup
  coarsely chopped macadamia nuts between
  each pan of popcorn.

- **Red and White Christmas Oven Caramel
  Corn:** Divide 2 cups dried cranberries and
  1 1/2 cups white baking chips between each
  pan of popcorn.

Oven Caramel Corn

Fudgy No-Bakes

PREP: 20 MIN; CHILL: 1 HR
36 SQUARES

1 3/4 cups graham cracker crumbs
(about 20 squares)

1 cup flaked coconut

1/4 cup baking cocoa

2 tablespoons granulated sugar

1/2 cup butter or margarine, melted

2 tablespoons water

2 cups powdered sugar

1/4 cup butter or margarine, softened

1 tablespoon milk

1 teaspoon vanilla

Candy decorations, if desired

Mix cracker crumbs, coconut, cocoa and granulated sugar in medium bowl. Stir in 1/2 cup
butter and the water. Press in ungreased square
pan, 9 × 9 × 2 inches. Refrigerate while preparing
topping.

Mix remaining ingredients except candy decorations. (If necessary, stir in additional 1 to 2 teaspoons milk until spreadable.) Spread over layer
in pan. Refrigerate 1 hour. Cut into 6 rows by
6 rows. Decorate with candy decorations. Store
loosely covered in refrigerator.

1 Square: Calories 95 (Calories from Fat 45); Fat 5g (Saturated 3g);
Cholesterol 10mg; Sodium 55mg; Carbohydrate 12g (Dietary Fiber 0g);
Protein 0g
% Daily Value: Vitamin A 2%; Vitamin C 0%; Calcium 0%; Iron 0%
Diet Exchanges: 1 Starch, 1/2 Fat

Fudgy No-Bakes

Timesaving Tips

You can save time (and mess) by purchasing already
crushed graham crackers at your supermarket.

Gifts for Giving

Get the whole family involved in making this
recipe the "family gift" for neighbors and friends.
Use decorator frostings to make wreaths and red
cinnamon candies for holly berries. Personalize
Fudgy No-Bakes by using decorator frosting to
write names or holiday greetings. Use disposable
aluminum pans to make gift giving a breeeze.

Christmas Mice Shortbread

PREP: 30 MIN; COOL: 1 HR

15 COOKIES

15 maraschino cherries with stems, drained

2/3 cup white baking chips or chocolate chips

1/2 teaspoon vegetable oil

1 package (5.3 ounces) shortbread triangles

30 sliced almonds

15 white baking chips or chocolate chips

Shredded coconut

15 red cinnamon candies

Cover work area with piece of waxed paper about 18 inches long. Dry cherries with paper towels.

Place 2/3 cup chips and the oil in 6-ounce custard cup. Microwave uncovered on High 1 minute to 1 minute 10 seconds or until chips are softened; stir until smooth.

Hold 1 cherry by stem (mouse tail), and dip into melted chips, covering completely. Immediately place on shortbread triangle, with tail at 45-degree angle. Place 2 of the sliced almonds against front of cherry to form mouse ears. Repeat with remaining cherries, shortbread and almonds.

Using the remaining melted chips as glue and a toothpick to spread the melted chips, attach the flat side of a whole chip (flat side back) to the base of the almonds to form the mouse head. Using melted chips as glue, attach a few shreds of coconut for the whiskers and a cinnamon candy for the nose.

Let cool without moving 50 to 60 minutes or until melted chip mixture is firm and completely set. Store in cool place up to 1 week.

1 Cookie: Calories 110 (Calories from Fat 55); Fat 6g (Saturated 2g); Cholesterol 2mg; Sodium 50mg; Carbohydrate 14g (Dietary Fiber 1g); Protein 1g
% Daily Value: Vitamin A 0%; Vitamin C 0%; Calcium 0%; Iron 4%
Diet Exchanges: 1 Fruit, 1 Fat

Holiday Hints

We think the shortbread cookies resemble a wedge of cheese, but you can use other purchased or homemade flat-surfaced cookies for the base of your mice decorations.

A merry mouse can add the final touch to your holiday food platters. Kids will have fun placing mice on a saucer next to Grandma and Grandpa's cups of coffee or on a plate of cookies for Santa.

Christmas Mice Shortbread

North Pole Strawberry Smoothie

PREP: 5 MIN
2 SERVINGS

1 package (10 ounces) frozen strawberries
   in syrup, partially thawed and undrained

1/4 cup water

2 cups vanilla frozen yogurt

2 tablespoons vanilla reduced-fat yogurt

1 strawberry-flavored or peppermint
   candy cane, about 6 inches long,
   finely crushed

Green decorating gel

Place strawberries and water in blender. Cover
and blend on medium-high speed until slushy.
Blend on medium speed until smooth. Transfer
to 2-cup measure.

Wash and dry blender. Place frozen yogurt and
reduced-fat yogurt in blender. Cover and blend
on medium speed until smooth.

Place crushed candy cane on small plate. Pipe
decorating gel around rim of two 12-ounce
glasses. Dip rims into crushed candy.

Carefully pour yogurt mixture and strawberries
at the same time into glasses, creating a half-
and-half design. Serve with large drinking straws
if desired.

1 Serving: Calories 425 (Calories from Fat 20); Fat 2g (Saturated 1g);
Cholesterol 10mg; Sodium 130mg; Carbohydrate 95g (Dietary
Fiber 3g); Protein 10g
% Daily Value: Vitamin A 2%; Vitamin C 100%; Calcium 32%;
Iron 6%
Diet Exchanges: 3 Starch, 3 Fruit

North Pole Strawberry Smoothie

Host a Santa's Breakfast for the neighborhood
kids! Here are a few helpful organizing tips:

- Send out invitations immediately after Thanksgiving.

- Limit the party to six guests, plus a couple par-
  ents you think could be helpful.

- Enlist a Santa (the earlier the better) to join the
  kids for breakfast.

- Have a small wrapped gift at each place setting
  or in Santa's sack to be distributed.

Christmas Vacation Peanut Butter Fondue

PREP: 10 MIN; COOK: 5 MIN
1 1/2 CUPS FONDUE

2/3 cup packed brown sugar

1/4 cup half-and-half

1 tablespoon honey

3/4 cup creamy peanut butter

Pieces of assorted cakes, candies and fruit, if desired (see Holiday Hints, below)

Heat brown sugar, half-and-half and honey to boiling in 2-quart saucepan over medium heat, stirring occasionally.

Stir in peanut butter until smooth. Pour into fondue pot or individual serving bowls. Dip assorted cakes, candies and fruit into fondue.

1/4 Cup: Calories 320 (Calories from Fat 160); Fat 18g (Saturated 4g); Cholesterol 5mg; Sodium 160mg; Carbohydrate 33g (Dietary Fiber 2g); Protein 8g
% Daily Value: Vitamin A 0%; Vitamin C 0%; Calcium 4%; Iron 6%
Diet Exchanges: 2 Starch, 3 1/2 Fat

Party Pointers

Have the Christmas Vacation Peanut Butter Fondue ready, and invite the neighbor kids to a children's holiday party. Activities could include cookie decorating.

Holiday Hints

To make fondue even more fun:

- Use chocolate-covered candy dessert sticks for dipping.
- Use sugar-cone sundae cups for individual-size fondue.
- Place chocolate sprinkles in a separate bowl into which to dip fondue-coated foods.

Try these tempting dippers:

- Purchased pound cake cut into cubes or seasonal shapes
- Animal crackers or graham cracker squares
- Marshmallows

- Strawberries, grapes, pineapple chunks, banana slices, apple slices and pear slices
- Small pretzel twists—plain or fudge-covered

Christmas Vacation Peanut Butter Fondue

Pineapple-Apricot Jam

PREP: 10 MIN; COOK: 12 MIN
ABOUT 5 HALF-PINTS JAM

1 jar (6 ounces) maraschino cherries, drained, and 1/3 cup syrup reserved

1 can (20 ounces) crushed pineapple in syrup, undrained

6 ounces dried apricots, cut into fourths (about 1 cup)

1/4 cup water

3 1/2 cups sugar

2 tablespoons lemon juice

1 pouch (3 ounces) liquid fruit pectin (from 6-ounce package)

Chop cherries; set aside. Heat reserved cherry syrup, the pineapple, apricots and water to boiling in Dutch oven, stirring occasionally; reduce heat. Cover and simmer about 10 minutes, stirring occasionally, until apricots are tender.

Stir in sugar, lemon juice and cherries. Heat to rolling boil over high heat, stirring occasionally. Boil and stir 1 minute; remove from heat. Stir in pectin.

Immediately pour mixture into hot, sterilized jars or freezer containers, leaving 1/2-inch headspace. Wipe rims of jars. Seal immediately; cool. Refrigerate or freeze up to 3 months. Thaw before serving.

1 Tablespoon: Calories 50 (Calories from Fat 0); Fat 0g (Saturated 0g); Cholesterol 0mg; Sodium 0mg; Carbohydrate 13g (Dietary Fiber 0g); Protein 0g
% Daily Value: Vitamin A 2%; Vitamin C 0%; Calcium 0%; Iron 0%
Diet Exchanges: 1 Fruit

Gifts for Giving

This brightly colored jam doesn't need much to say Merry Christmas all by itself. Simply:

- Use fancy cut-glass jars and homemade decorative labels to add that holiday sparkle.

- Top it off with a piece of decorative fabric or paper, and tie with a matching ribbon.

Pineapple-Apricot Jam

Spicy Mocha Mix

PREP: 10 MIN
ABOUT 1 CUP MIX (24 SERVINGS)

1/2 cup sugar

1/4 cup instant coffee (dry)

1/4 cup baking cocoa

1 teaspoon ground nutmeg

1/2 teaspoon ground cinnamon

Stir all ingredients until completely mixed. Store in tightly covered container at room temperature up to 6 months.

For each serving: Place 2 to 3 teaspoons mix in cup or mug and fill with 2/3 cup boiling water; stir. Top with whipped cream if desired. For 6 servings, place 1/4 to 1/3 cup mix in heat-proof container and add 4 cups boiling water.

1 Serving: Calories 20 (Calories from Fat 0); Fat 0g (Saturated 0g); Cholesterol 0mg; Sodium 0mg; Carbohydrate 5g (Dietary Fiber 0g); Protein 0g
% Daily Value: Vitamin A 0%; Vitamin C 0%; Calcium 0%; Iron 0%
Diet Exchanges: Not recommended

JAVA MIX: Decrease cocoa to 2 tablespoons and omit nutmeg and cinnamon.

ORANGE CAFÉ AU LAIT MIX: Omit cocoa and nutmeg. Add 1/2 cup powdered nondairy creamer and 1 teaspoon grated orange peel.

Spicy Mocha Mix and Easy Festive Peppermint Marshmallows (page 42)

Gifts for Giving

Any busy friend will love a "pampering package." Fill a basket with a large holiday mug, jars of Spicy Mocha Mix, Java Mix and Orange Café au Lait Mix, a package of biscotti, a relaxation audio tape or a new book off the best-seller list.

Easy Festive Peppermint Marshmallows

PREP: 5 MIN; COOK: 10 MIN; STAND: 8 HR

ABOUT 40 MARSHMALLOWS

Powdered sugar

2 1/2 tablespoons unflavored gelatin

1/2 cup cold water

1 1/2 cups granulated sugar

1 cup corn syrup

1/4 teaspoon salt

1/2 cup water

1 teaspoon peppermint extract

Generously dust rectangular baking dish, 11 × 7 1/2 × 2 inches, with powdered sugar. Sprinkle gelatin on 1/2 cup cold water in large bowl to soften; set aside.

Heat granulated sugar, corn syrup, salt and 1/2 cup water in 2-quart saucepan over low heat, stirring constantly, until sugar is dissolved. Heat to boiling; cook without stirring to 250° on candy thermometer or until small amount of mixture dropped into very cold water forms a ball that holds its shape but is pliable; remove from heat.

Slowly pour syrup into softened gelatin while beating with electric mixer on high speed. Beat on high speed until mixture is white and has almost tripled in volume. Add peppermint extract; beat on high speed 1 minute. Pour into pan. Sprinkle with powdered sugar, patting lightly with hands. Let stand uncovered at least 8 hours.

Turn pan upside down to remove marshmallow mixture onto board. Cut into shapes with miniature cookie cutters or knife dipped in water to keep from sticking. Store in airtight container at room temperature up to 3 weeks.

1 Marshmallow: Calories 55 (Calories from Fat 0); Fat 0g (Saturated 0g); Cholesterol 0mg; Sodium 25mg; Carbohydrate 14g (Dietary Fiber 0g); Protein 0g
% Daily Value: Vitamin A 0%; Vitamin C 0%; Calcium 0%; Iron 0%
Diet Exchanges: 1 Fruit

See photo on page 41.

Gifts for Giving

Package a collection of marshmallows in a plastic bag, and tie with curly ribbon. Place bags of marshmallows in oversized mugs along with packages of gourmet cocoa.

Holiday Hints

Check out the cookie and canapé cutters in craft and gourmet kitchen stores for fun new shapes. For more holiday flair, drizzle marshmallows with melted vanilla candy coating tinted with paste food color. You may want to let marshmallows air-dry, and then string them on fancy cord as holiday garland.

Salt Dough Decorations

PREP: 30 MIN; BAKE: 2 HR PER SHEET; COOL: 30 MIN
ABOUT 5 DOZEN 2 1/2-INCH DECORATIONS

4 cups all-purpose flour

2 cups salt

1 1/2 cups water

1 teaspoon powdered alum

Clear sealing spray for crafts, if desired

Mix all ingredients thoroughly with hands. (If dough is too dry, work in 1 tablespoon water.) If desired, tint dough by dividing into several parts and kneading desired food color into each part. Roll or mold dough as directed below. Cover and refrigerate dough up to 2 weeks

To roll: Roll dough 1/8 inch thick on lightly floured surface. Cut with cookie cutters. If making ornaments to be hung, make a hole in each 1/4 inch from top with end of plastic straw.

To mold: Shape dough, no more than 1/2 inch thick, into figures such as flowers, fruits, vegetables or animals. If making ornaments to be hung, insert fine wire in each.

Heat oven to 250°. Place decorations on ungreased cookie sheet. Bake 30 minutes. Remove from oven; turn decorations over (if possible). Bake about 1 1/2 hours longer or until completely hard and dry. Remove from cookie sheet to wire rack; cool completely.

Lightly sand flat surfaces of decorations with fine sandpaper until smooth. Outline desired designs on decorations with pencil. Paint with plastic-based poster or acrylic paint. (Paint sides and backs of ornaments, too.) Let stand until paint is dry. Place decorations on waxed paper. Spray with sealing spray.

FOR DECORATION ONLY. NOT EDIBLE.

Holiday Hints

Kids will have fun using this easy-to-make dough to create place cards, ornaments or tabletop decorations. Here are a few tips to help with your merry making:

- Use whole wheat flour for the all-purpose flour to craft teddy bears, mice and natural-colored decorations.

- Press dough through a garlic press to produce textures for hair, animal fur, grass and greenery for wreaths and trees.

- Brush dough with slightly beaten egg white before baking for a glossy surface.

- Brush dough with milk before baking for a golden brown color.

Salt Dough Decorations

Cranberry Kissing Ball

PREP: 45 MIN
1 DECORATION

12 inches 20-gauge wire

1 plastic foam ball, 3 inches in diameter

Round toothpicks

1/2 pound fresh cranberries

1 small bunch (about 5 sprigs) fresh eucalyptus

1 package craft straight pins

1 yard decorative ribbon

Cranberry Kissing Ball

Wrap wire tightly around diameter of foam ball once. Twist wire at top of ball to secure. Tuck ends into ball.

Break toothpicks in half. Push cranberry onto broken end of toothpick; push other end of toothpick into foam ball. Continue until ball is well filled with cranberries.

Fill in open spaces on ball with 1 1/2- to 2-inch cuts of eucalyptus, securing with pins.

Slip ribbon through wire twist at top; tie ribbon to make loop for hanging ball. The cranberries will stay plump and pretty for about three to four days. To extend its life, hang the ball in a cool spot, such as in an entryway or on a porch.

New Twist

Hanging in an entryway, a kissing ball welcomes guests with a romantic touch. Instead of eucalyptus, you may like to add mistletoe or holly for a hint of Christmas past or, if you're not fond of eucalyptus, use popped popcorn to fill in the open spaces between cranberries.

Holiday Hints

Having trouble finding craft straight pins? Look for them in the notions department of sewing and fabric stores.

Helpful Nutrition and Cooking Information

Nutrition Guidelines

We provide nutrition information for each recipe that includes calories, fat, cholesterol, sodium, carbohydrate, fiber and protein. Individual food choices can be based on this information.

Recommended intake for a daily diet of 2,000 calories as set by the Food and Drug Administration:

Total Fat	Less than 65g
Saturated Fat	Less than 20g
Cholesterol	Less than 300mg
Sodium	Less than 2,400mg
Total Carbohydrate	300g
Dietary Fiber	25g

Criteria Used for Calculating Nutrition Information

- The first ingredient was used wherever a choice is given (such as 1/3 cup sour cream or plain yogurt).
- The first ingredient amount was used wherever a range is given (such as 3- to 3-1/2–pound cut-up broiler-fryer chicken).
- The first serving number was used wherever a range is given (such as 4 to 6 servings).
- "If desired" ingredients and recipe variations were not included (such as sprinkle with brown sugar, if desired).
- Only the amount of a marinade or frying oil that is estimated to be absorbed by the food during preparation or cooking was calculated.

Ingredients Used in Recipe Testing and Nutrition Calculations

- Ingredients used for testing represent those that the majority of consumers use in their homes: large eggs, 2% milk, 80%-lean ground beef, canned ready-to-use chicken broth and vegetable oil spread containing not less than 65 percent fat.
- Fat-free, low-fat or low-sodium products were not used, unless otherwise indicated.
- Solid vegetable shortening (not butter, margarine, nonstick cooking sprays or vegetable oil spread as they can cause sticking problems) was used to grease pans, unless otherwise indicated.

Equipment Used in Recipe Testing

We use equipment for testing that the majority of consumers use in their homes. If a specific piece of equipment (such as a wire whisk) is necessary for recipe success, it is listed in the recipe.

- Cookware and bakeware without nonstick coatings were used, unless otherwise indicated.
- No dark-colored, black or insulated bakeware was used.
- When a pan is specified in a recipe, a metal pan was used; a baking dish or pie plate means ovenproof glass was used.
- An electric hand mixer was used for mixing only when mixer speeds are specified in the recipe directions. When a mixer speed is not given, a spoon or fork was used.

INDEX

NOTE: Page numbers in *italics* indicate a photograph.

Appetizer, 8–11
  Cheese Trees, 8, *9*; variation
    Snowman, 8, *9*
  Ginger Shrimp Kabobs, 10, *11*
Apple(s)
  Applesauce-Sweet Potato Bake,
    20, *20*
  -Caramel Oven Caramel Corn,
    34, *34*
  Applesaazuce-Sweet Potato Bake,
    20, *20*
Apricot, Pineapple- Jam, 40, *40*

Baked Ham, Glazed, 14, *15*;
    carving, 14; sauces for, 15
Bean, Three- Christmas Chili, 17, *17*
Beef Stew, Burgundy, 12, *13*
Beverage, 6–7, 37, 41. See also
    Drink
Biscuits, Pesto, 28, *29*
Bourbon Balls (candies), 33
Bread, Holiday, 26–29
  Julekake (with mixed candied
    fruit), 26, *27*; variation,
    using bread machine, 26
  Pesto Biscuits, 28, *29*
Bread Pudding, Peanut Brittle, 25,
    25; Hot Buttered Rum
    Sauce for, 25
Broccoli-Corn Casserole, 21, *21*
Brownies. See Fudgy No-Bakes
Burgundy Beef Stew, 12, *13*
Butter Rum Glaze, 30

Café au Lait, 41
Cake, 22–24.
  Cheesecake, Heavenly, 24, *24*
  Fruitcake, Jeweled, 22, *23*;
    variations, 22

Candy(ies), 32–34. See also
    Cookies
  Caramel Corn, Oven, 34, *34*;
    variations: Caramel-Apple;
    Hawaiian; Red and White
    Christmas, 34
  Chocolate-Wine Balls, 33, *33*;
    variations: Bourbon; Rum;
    White Wine, 33
  Peppermint Bark, 32, *32*;
    variations, 32
Cappuccino Eggnog, Hot, 6, *7*
Caramel(s)
  -Apple Oven Caramel Corn, 34
  Corn, Oven, 34, *34*; variations:
    Caramel-Apple; Hawaiian;
    Red and White Christmas, 34
Casserole
  Applesauce-Sweet Potato Bake,
    20, *20*
  Broccoli-Corn, 21, *21*
  Chicken Dijon, 16, *16*
Cheese Trees, Appetizer, 20, *21*;
    variation, Snowman, 20
Cheesecake, Heavenly, 24, *24*
Chicken Dijon Casserole, 16, *16*
Chili, Three-Bean Christmas, 17, *17*
Chocolate.
  Fudgy No-Bakes, 35, *35*
  Spicy Mocha Mix (drink), 41
  Spritz, 30
  -Wine Balls, 33, *33*; variations:
    Bourbon; Rum; White
    Wine, 33
Cinnamon Cider, 7, *7*
Cherry Sauce, Sour, 15
Christmas Mice Shortbread, 36
Christmas Vacation Peanut Butter
    Fondue, 38, *39*

Coffee. See Cappuccino; Spicy
    Mocha Mix
Cookies, 30–31, 35, 36. See also
    Candy
  Fudgy No-Bakes, 35, *35*
  Shortbread, Christmas Mice, 36, *36*
  Spritz, Holiday, 30, *31*; variations:
    Chocolate; Rum Butter;
    Spicy, 30
Cooking and nutrition information,
    45
Corn, Broccoli- Casserole, 21, *21*
Cranberry Kissing Ball
    (decoration), 44

Decorations, 43–44. See also Gifts
  Cranberry, Kissing Ball, 44, *44*
  Salt Dough, 43, *43*
Dessert, 22–25. See also Cake;
    Chocolate; Fondue;
    Pudding
Dijon Chicken Casserole, 16, *16*
Drink, 6–7, 36, 41
  Cinnamon Cider, 7, *7*
  Eggnog, Holiday, 6, *7*; variation,
    Hot Cappuccino, 6
  Spicy Mocha Mix, 41
  Strawberry Smoothie, North
    Pole, 37, *37*

Eggnog, Holiday, 6, *7*; variation,
    Hot Cappuccino, 6
Easy Festive Peppermint
    Marshmallows, 42

Fondue, Peanut Butter, Christmas
    Vacation, 38, *39*; dippers
    for, 38

Fruit
  Salad, Heavenly, 18, *19*
  Cranberry Kissing Ball (decoration),
    44, *44*
Fruitcake, Jeweled, 22, *23*;
    variations, 22
Fudgy No-Bakes (cookies), 35, *35*

Gifts. See also Decorations
  candies in a wine glass, 33, *33*
  caramel corn gift bags, 34
  casserole dish filled with special
    recipe, 21
  drink mix assortment, 41
  fruitcakes, petite or mini-loaves,
    22, *23*
  Fudgy No-Bakes, personalized, 35
  Jam, Pineapple-Apricot, 40, *40*
  marshmallow collection, 42
Ginger Shrimp Kabobs, 10, *11*
Glazed Baked Ham, 14, *15*;
    carving, 14; sauces for, 15

Ham, Glazed Baked, 14, *15*;
    carving, 14; sauces for, 15
Hawaiian Oven Caramel Corn, 34
Heavenly Cheesecake, 24, *24*
Heavenly Fruit Salad, 18, *18*
Holiday Eggnog, 6, *7*
Holiday Spritz, 30, *31*
Honey, Orange- Dressing (for fruit
    salad), 18
Honey mustard and sour cream
    sauce, 15
Hot Buttered Rum Sauce, 25
Hot Drinks
  Cappuccino Eggnog, 6
  Spicy Mocha Mix, 41, *41*

Ingredients used in recipes, 45

Jam, Pineapple-Apricot 40, *40*
Java Mix (drink), 41
Jeweled Fruitcake, 22, *23*;
    variations, 22
Julekake (with mixed candied
    fruit), 26, *27*; variation,
    using bread machine, 26

Kabobs, Ginger Shrimp, 10, *11*
Kissing Ball, Cranberry
    (decoration), 44, *44*

Main dishes, 12–16
Marshmallows, Peppermint, Easy
    Festive, 41, *42*
Mini-loaves (fruitcake), 22, *23*
Mocha. See also Cappucino
  Mix, Spicy, 41, *41*; variations:
    Java; Orange Café au Lait, 41
Mustard, honey sauce, 15

No-Bakes, Fudgy, 35, *35*
North Pole Strawberry Smoothie,
    37, *37*
Nutrition and cooking information,
    45

Orange Café au Lait Mix (drink), 41
Orange-Honey Dressing (for fruit
    salad), 18
Oven Caramel Corn, 34, *34*;
    variations: Caramel-Apple;
    Hawaiian; Red and White
    Christmas, 34

Party Pointers (ideas for parties)
  name tags, 10
  Santa's breakfast, 37
  slow cooker, using, 7
  tree-trimming, 17
Pasta. See Chicken Dijon Casserole
Peanut Brittle Bread Pudding, 25,
    25; Hot Buttered Rum
    Sauce for, 25
Peanut Butter Fondue, Christmas
    Vacation, 38, *39*; dippers
    for, 38
Peppermint
  Bark, 32, *32*; variations, 32
  Marshmallows, Easy Festive, 42
Pesto Biscuits, 28, *29*
Pineapple-Apricot Jam, 40, *40*
Pomegranate seeds, adding to
    salad, 18
Popcorn, Oven Caramel Corn, 34,
    34; variations: Caramel-
    Apple; Hawaiian; Red and
    White Christmas, 34

Pork. See Ham
Pudding, Bread, Peanut Brittle, 25,
    25; Hot Buttered Rum
    Sauce for, 25

Raisin Sauce, 15
Red and White Christmas Oven
    Caramel Corn, 34
Rum
  Balls (candies), 33
  Butter Spritz (cookies), 30
  Hot Buttered, 25, *25*; Sauce, 25

Salad, Fruit, Heavenly, 18, *19*
Salt Dough Decorations, 43, *43*
Sauce(s).
  for Baked Ham, 15
  Honey, Orange- Dressing (for
    fruit salad), 18
  honey mustard and sour cream, 15
  Hot Buttered Rum, 25
  Raisin, 15
  Sour Cherry, 15
Seafood. See Shrimp
Shortbread cookies, Christmas
    Mice, 36, *36*
Shrimp Kabobs, Ginger, 10, *11*
Side Dishes, 20–21. See also Salad
Smoothie, Strawberry, North Pole,
    37, *37*
Snowman Cheese Ball, 8, *9*
Spicy
  Mocha Mix (drink), 41
  Spritz (cookies), 30, *31*
Spritz (cookies), Holiday, 30, *31*;
    variations: Chocolate; Rum
    Butter; Spicy, 30
Stew, Beef, Burgundy, 12, *13*
Strawberry Smoothie, North Pole,
    37, *37*
Sweet Potato, Applesauce- Bake,
    20, *20*

Three-Bean Christmas Chili, 17, *17*

White Wine Balls (candies), 33, *33*
Wine, Chocolate- Balls (candies),
    33, *33*; variations: Rum or
    Bourbon; White Wine, 33